Finding Your
Strength in
Difficult Times

Finding Your Strength in Difficult Times

A BOOK OF MEDITATIONS

David Viscott

New York Chicago San Francisco Lisbon London Madrid Mexico City
Milan New Delhi San Juan Seoul Singapore Sydney Toronto

Library of Congress Cataloging-in-Publication Data

Viscott, David S., 1938–
 Finding your strength in difficult times : a book of meditations /
David Viscott.
   p. cm.
  ISBN 0-07-141863-6
  1. Spiritual life—Meditations. I. Title.

BL624.2.V57 1993
242'.4—dc20
                  93-04927
                  CIP

16 17 18 19 20 21 QVS/QVS 21 20 19 18 17

ISBN-13: 978-0-07-141863-8
ISBN-10: 0-07-141863-6

This book is printed on acid-free paper.

For Bill Young

Contents

🐌

Introduction

❧

Everyone is looking for happiness.
But happiness is not a goal. It
is a result of doing what you like and
relating honestly to other people.

Happiness is about being your own
person, making your own decisions,
doing what you want because you want
to do it, and living your own life to
please yourself. It's about being inde-
pendent, allowing others to be free, and
seeking the best in yourself and in the
world.

It's so easy to do the opposite—to
cling to others expecting to be taken
care of, to control people and blame
them when things go wrong, to be insincere and play at relationships and
careers rather than commit, to tease
rather than respond, and to live on the

fringe of others' lives rather than in the middle of your own.

When you do not live your life as your own person, you live an unhappy life indeed. You have the sense that your life is going nowhere, that life has little meaning, and that the meaning it does have loses its substance when you examine it closely.

Your life is supposed to be for yourself.

Your life is given to you to create its meaning. You have no one to blame if your life does not turn out the way you wanted it to be. No one owes you anything. You are the only person who can make a lasting difference. A little boost of support here or there means nothing unless you have committed to go all the way yourself, no matter what happens.

No promises that anyone ever

made to you have the power to make a lasting difference.

No betrayal or abandonment has the power to limit your growth or blunt your success unless you need an excuse for failing that badly.

Putting it bluntly, you have the ability to get over just about everything. And if you intend to be happy during this life you are going to have to get over a lot all the time.

The first thing you have to get over is the belief that someone is coming in your life who is going to make all the difference.

Don't count on anyone coming to rescue you, give you the big break, defeat your enemies, stand up for you, recognize your worth, and open doors.

Either you are the savior in your own life or your life is without redemption.

You deserve to be happy, but you also deserve everything that you accept. So look at your unhappiness. It is a record of your failure to be your own person.

Your unhappiness is really nothing more than a reminder that you have some work to do to be happy again.

Because being happy is liking the way you feel; if you are unhappy it means that you don't like the way you feel.

You are the person who is supposed to do something about that.

Being happy requires that you take subtle but important risks all the time.

You need to assert yourself. Avoid manipulation, pointless arguments, and confrontations.

You need to tell the truth and correct your lies.

You need to stop playing the victim so you can enjoy your success without feeling guilty.

To find happiness you need to be your own person, not a pretender.

You need to let go of your expectations of what you think life should be like so that you don't unrealistically judge others and find them lacking and ungiving.

You need to give up living in the past.

You need to learn to forgive and to let go in order to move on.

You need to learn to listen in order to bring out the best in others.

You need to take yourself seriously, but not so seriously that you have to be perfect all the time or cannot admit your errors or weaknesses.

You need to understand that you are always growing. So you must continually be aware of the compromises that inhibit your growth and the relationships where you feel you give away too much.

You need a purpose in life.

You need to work at that purpose and create the life you want, not live in empty hope of deliverance.

Being happy takes work, the work of life. Since you are going to live your own life, you might as well live it as your best.

Each of the sections that follow addresses one particular issue on the road to becoming your own person and finding happiness. It is all straightforward advice and has common sense and directness to recommend it. Most of it you already know. It is presented in this fashion to inspire you to accept yourself so that you can find and give your gift.

This is a concentrated book of

knowledge, and many important meanings may slip by you on first reading. Whether you read a page a day or read this book in one sitting, each of these pages deserves rereading.

You will discover that the way you see the individual sections will change as you grow or when your situation changes.

Sometimes it takes a crisis to open you up to a new understanding or allow you to incorporate this advice into your life. Going back over a section in a time of difficulty will open you up to new ideas that you may have missed before.

I urge you to take all of this to heart. I have assembled it from a lifetime of working with people. I have written it so that it cuts through to the center of each issue and speaks directly to your heart.

Being happy is understanding and accepting yourself as you are right now.

That is the only true freedom.

This, the only time to achieve it.

You, the only person who can do it.

Being Happy

Being happy is liking the way you feel and being open to the future without fear.

Being happy is accepting yourself at this place and time.

Being happy is not being perfect, becoming rich, falling in love, having power, knowing the right people, or succeeding in your job.

Being happy is liking yourself the way you are right now—maybe not all of yourself, but the essential you.

You deserve to love yourself for the way you are at this moment.

If you think you have to be more than you are now to be happy and love yourself, you are imposing impossible conditions on yourself.

Only you know yourself the way

you do. You can compile the longest and least sympathetic inventory of your faults. At any time, no matter how successful or accomplished you become, you will be able to undermine your happiness by reciting this list of faults.

Know your faults but don't allow their existence to become an excuse for not loving yourself just the way you are.

🐢

**Knowing that my best can only come from me,
I accept myself just as I am.**

Be Your Own Person

❧

People who say they cannot be their own person usually claim that someone else is keeping them from being themselves.

How can that be true? How can you be anyone but yourself?

When you are afraid to risk, you stop being your own person. Then you become the ward of anyone who will protect you.

Unfortunately, the person who protects you expects you to behave like the person he or she feels you should be, the person he or she rescued you to become.

If you're afraid of being your own person, you're probably afraid of taking care of yourself or being on your own.

If someone should want to accompany you, fine; but the purpose of choosing your own way is to keep company with your own best, not to rely on the strength of others.

Accept your independence and the loneliness that comes with it by being willing to go it alone, not in defiance, but as a choice.

If you're afraid of being your own person, you're probably afraid of your anger. You feel you have to hold it in or else you might offend the person you depend on for your survival, or run the risk of being thrown out in the cold if you express yourself.

So you hold your anger inside, and after a time it turns inward. Then you hate yourself for being weak, inferior, not being your own person.

It's a vicious cycle.

You're never trapped if you're your own person.

You may make mistakes, but you're free to correct them.

You may hurt others, but you are able to apologize and deal with their rejection.

You may be hurt, but you feel strong enough to love again.

Save yourself.

Just do what's right for you.

Express yourself.

Find your life and live it.

If you cannot act in your own best interests, you cannot act in anyone else's.

I am my own person.
I am only my own person.
I am enough.

Peace of Mind

❧

Peace of mind is knowing that you did what you had to do and forgiving yourself when you weren't as strong as you wanted to be.

Peace of mind is an easy thing.

When you have to work at it, you do not find peace of mind, because the peace of mind you work for is too fragile, too tentative.

Peace of mind needs to be present before your good work, not the result of it.

If you can accept that you have good intentions, you can have peace of mind.

You can have peace of mind before forgiving, if you are sincere and intend to forgive.

You can have peace of mind before

setting right a difficult situation if you are determined in your intention.

Peace of mind is the acceptance of your good and your intention to do the right thing.

If you have to accomplish something to have peace of mind, even if it is making good on damage you have done to others or keeping promises, your peace of mind is only fleeting.

True peace of mind is knowing that you will do what you need to do and believing in your goodness and your power to do it.

I do good.
I intend good.
I am good.

Accept Yourself

❧

When you don't accept yourself, you become oversensitive to rejection.

When you don't accept yourself, you lose faith every time you trip over an old weakness.

When you don't accept yourself, you waste time looking for love to make you complete.

When you don't accept yourself, you try to beat others rather than seeking your best.

When you don't accept yourself, you overvalue material things.

When you don't accept yourself, you always feel lonely, and being with other people doesn't seem to help.

When you don't accept yourself, you live in the past.

Acceptance is not a hopeless position; it's the only position from which you can grow.

If you accept all of your life, none of it will have been wasted.

When you don't accept yourself, you dread what each day may reveal about you.

When you don't accept yourself, the truth becomes your enemy.

When you don't accept yourself, you have no place to hide.

Accepting yourself is everything.

If you accept yourself, you can accept the world.

❧

I accept all of the parts of who I am.
What I cannot accept, I forgive.

What Other People
Think

❧

What other people think is only what other people think.

Other people are just as confused as you are, just as insecure, just as frightened, just as likely to make mistakes, to be envious, jealous, or self-deceiving, and, therefore, just as likely to distort what they hear and see.

First of all, what other people think about you is none of your business.

Remember that.

But if you must know what other people think, it has more to do about how they feel about themselves than how they feel about you.

Other people are probably wondering what you think of them.

Think about that.

❧

What I think of myself is all that matters.
I value myself.
I remember my goodness.

Please Yourself

❧

If you are going to die your own death, you might as well live your own life.

Whenever you try to please other people, you make their feelings more important than your own.

If you postpone your pleasure and always put others first, even if you think you are doing so out of love, you end up being disappointed in their response to you.

Somehow it's never enough when you try to please others, for you or for them.

You end up expecting too much. This leads to resentment.

Soon life loses its pleasure, because you depend on other people to make you happy, and you don't believe anyone truly can.

No one knows how to please you the way you know how to please yourself.

❧

**I please myself and put my feelings first.
I deserve to be happy just for myself.**

Be a Little Selfish

If you sacrifice yourself hoping that others will reward you, you are only fooling yourself and setting up other people to disappoint you.

If you do not do what you need to do to make yourself happy, who should?

If you are not a happy person and are waiting for something to happen to make your life better, you will wait a long time.

Your job is to make your life happy.

There is something that you want to do that you can do right now.

Do it.

Other people won't think you are selfish.

Other people probably won't even notice.

If they do notice, most likely they will envy you.

Besides, what do you owe anyone who argues with you for making yourself happy?

If someone is going to hate you no matter what you do, you might as well do whatever you want.

🐚

**I am for myself so that I can be happy.
I am for myself so that I can give freely to others.**

Don't Wait for
Love

❧

If another person is going to love you,
that person already loves you and
there is nothing you need to do to win
that love.

If people tell you that the reason
they don't love you is because you don't
do something for them, such as obey
them or meet their expectations, the
sad truth is that they will not love you
when you follow their commands or
meet those expectations.

Such love is conditional.

People who offer conditional love
want to control you. The moment that
they give their love without condition is
the moment you are free.

This is not what they want.

So when you please someone in

order to get his or her love, you will soon discover that that love is not worth having, or that new conditions have been added for you to meet before you are loved.

When you want to be loved, you neglect to acknowledge the love that already exists.

❧

I give love freely and expect nothing in return.

Recognize When
You Are Loved

•

The person who loves you loves you
because he or she loves you.

That's it. No further explanations
are needed.

No explanations make sense of
love anyway.

When there is a powerful reason, a
burning need for someone to love you,
then the love that results is precarious
and can suddenly disappear.

The people who cling to you may
make you feel secure, even powerful at
first, but in time their love will smother
you and you'll reject them.

The people who rescue you will
end up controlling you, and you'll
come to hate yourself for being weak
and susceptible to being bought off so
cheaply.

The people who flatter you act on the belief that you cannot tell the difference between real love and fawning. They insult your intelligence, and you only believe them when you are desperately insecure.

The love that is most powerful exists for itself, without reasons, conditions, or excuses.

When you find someone who loves you because of the person you are, the way you do things, your humor, your personality, or because this person likes the way he or she feels about himself or herself in your presence, be true to this person.

This person mirrors your best.

🐘

I do not try to be accepted.
I do not search for love.
I want only to be me and am grateful
for the gift of myself.

Don't Be
Manipulated

❧

Everyone who is manipulated feels the same way about it.

When you are manipulated, you often feel that you need to make an excuse just for being the way you are.

The explanation is simple. When you are manipulated, you feel as if you have been treated unfairly.

When you are manipulated, someone is trying to control you.

Someone does not want you to be free to have your own opinions, express your own feelings, or make your own decisions.

When you are manipulated, you feel intimidated.

You feel hesitant about doing what you want to do, what you would do if you were simply being your natural self and acting the way you wanted, the way you do when you are with yourself.

When you feel manipulated, just do what you want to do. Be natural about it. Don't make a big thing out of it.

Just say, "I'm doing what I want. Is there anything wrong with that?"

And do it without looking back or asking permission.

If someone does not want you to please yourself, why should you even bother to listen?

I do what I want to do because I want to do it.

When Your Friends Succeed

❧

We all wish our friends well, but not *that* well.

Don't be put off by this. You're only human. You want your friends to succeed, but when they do and you are not sure of yourself, you fear being shown up.

When you feel down about yourself, it's easier to tolerate hearing about a friend's misfortunes than his or her successes.

Because your friends are closest to being like you, their success makes you question yourself.

"Why not me?" you ask. We all feel this way.

Nothing alienates people quite like success.

When people become successful, they discover a sad and unexpected truth:

It is lonely at the top.

Your friends need to celebrate their success without feeling that they are intimidating you and to share their failures without your taking secret satisfaction from them.

Allow your friends to confide their success in you without becoming envious of it or asking to participate in it.

Just say, "No one deserved it more."

You'll probably be right.

You'll certainly be a friend.

❧

I am happy for my friends' happiness. Sharing their happiness is my happiness.

Be a Friend

❧

Friends share the same vulnerability. People often become friends when they suffer through a difficult situation together.

People become friends because they share the same losses, the same desperation . . . and the same precariousness.

Friends often share the same risk, for fear bonds people together.

This is not difficult to understand. A person is either closed or open in the face of danger.

When fear is great, most people are transparent.

You make friends with the people whose emotional reaction you can understand, whose empathy seems genuine.

If you are unsure of yourself, you may reject the friends you made during times of adversity because they remind you of your own weakness or terror.

Recognize that your friendships celebrate your vulnerability and are proof of your humanness.

In a true friendship there is no need to hide.

Nor any place to hide, either.

❧

**I care about my friend's feelings.
I take the time to listen.
I hear myself within my friend.
I allow my friend to hear me.**

Find Something to
Be Grateful For

You can make a case for the sky falling if you want.

Perhaps your argument will be true in one instance, but negative logic really doesn't hold up over the long run.

Negative logic is almost always false, even though you could reason that there is always something bad happening to you all the time.

There is always something good happening as well.

It gets a little hard to see it when you are only focused on the negative.

The world is neither good nor bad. At best it is neutral.

You make the case that your unresolved pain demands.

When you are afraid, you find things to fear all around you.

When you are hurt, you see suffering and hopelessness.

When you are angry, you discern plots and enemies lurking everywhere.

When you feel guilty, you seek out disappointment and take it as well-deserved punishment and lose your will to grow.

Of course, while all of this negativity is going on, something good is also taking place.

Find that good.

Be grateful for finding it.

Your seeking the good is the greatest good you'll find.

I am grateful for music.
I am grateful for the stars.
I thank flowers.
Being is my reward.

Let Go

You were hurt.

Badly hurt.

Someone you trusted betrayed you.

Your plans fell through.

You took a risk and lost.

What are you going to do about it?

Seek revenge, live in an angry fantasy, eat your heart out?

If there is peace to be made, make it, but not at the price of hiding your hurt or pretending that everything is OK.

You need to let go of what doesn't work for you.

Risk admitting what you already know in your heart.

Learn whatever lesson there is to

learn from your loss, what matters and what makes no difference.

Save what can be saved.

Let go of what is never going to be.

Holding onto the impossible is the source of most of your pain.

Remember, in the end, suffering is just another choice.

**I open my hand and release the
world.
I am here.
I am all I need.**

Be a Little Braver

❧

The truth is, it's not going to take that much to make your life better.

Just a little effort.

You don't need to climb Mount Everest; you just need to take one little step.

Be a little braver.

The diet you are struggling with will succeed if you are just a little braver.

The job you are working on will be fine if you find the courage to work just a little harder.

The task you dread, the grades you wish to accomplish, the difficult time you need to get through can all be handled if you act a little braver.

You don't have to solve all of your problems.

You just have to begin.
Be a little braver.

I am ready.
I am now.
I can.
I will.

Don't Pretend That You Are Perfect

❧

Anyone who knows you knows that you're not perfect.

As a matter of fact, no one knows anyone who is perfect.

You only think people can be perfect when you're a kid. You probably thought your parents were perfect in order to believe they could rescue you from any danger.

It is a painful discovery to learn that your parents are only human.

You may have felt that you needed to be perfect to be worthy of your parents' love.

That's understandable, but it may be hard to admit that your parents' love was not enough to make you feel lovable just the way you are.

Maybe you felt that unless you were perfect, someone would withdraw their love and abandon you.

The fear lurking within everyone who tries to be perfect is the fear of not being lovable.

What are you going to do about that?

You are never going to be perfect. And none of the people you thought were perfect ever were.

Give up being perfect.

Maybe you need to love yourself, warts and all.

Admitting your imperfections makes you lovable.

🐦

**Here I am, flaws and all.
Waiting for nothing, giving my love.**

Be Sincere

I nsincerity is trying to get away with as much as you can.

Most insincerity is the result of trying to please others, especially when you're afraid you won't be liked if you speak the truth or say how you really feel.

Don't pretend to care about something when you really don't care at all. It just sets people up to expect what you have no intention of delivering. Remember your manners, but be straightforward just the same.

People will dislike you more for misleading them than if you hurt them openly.

When people are aware you hurt them, they can protect themselves and limit the damage. When you deceive them, you lull them into a false sense of security and lower their guard. The damage you do is greater because it is tainted with your betrayal.

Say what you really mean. You may risk rejection if you do, but it's better than hating yourself for using others.

When you are insincere, you become insensitive to others and unaware when you hurt or use them. Worse, you justify your actions by claiming that you're only doing what others would do if they were in your position.

When you try to convince yourself that everyone is just as superficial as you, the loveliness of the world fades and nothing seems to matter or have meaning.

When others depend on your

strength, it is your sincerity they are counting upon.

❧

**I mean to make a difference.
I act in accordance with my intentions.
I have nothing to hide.**

Do What *You* Want

❧

The only explanation you ever need for doing what you want is: "I want to."

The only explanation you ever need for not doing what you don't want to do is: "I don't want to."

The people who love you will understand.

The people who do not will not.

You do not need to convince anyone of anything. Actually, you can't convince people who want to control you of anything.

State your preferences directly and openly.

Think of this for a moment. The people who oppose your decision are only stating their opinion, their preferences. Why is their opinion about your life more important than your opinion about your own?

You wouldn't object if others did what they wanted to do. You might not like it or agree, but you recognize other people are free to live their lives any way they like. Just like you! It's only fair.

Memorize these two explanations: "I want to" and "I don't want to."

You don't need excuses to be yourself.

❧

I make myself happy by doing what I please.

Pay Your Own Way

❧

Here's an interesting idea. It has some wonderful benefits.

Pay your own way. You won't owe anyone anything. Anything!

You won't be compromised by the fear of disappointing people. Other people's expectations will simply be their expectations, not your obligation.

You can make your own decisions: where to go, what to do, where to stay, what to eat, when to leave, and when to remain home. You can say no without feeling guilty and yes without feeling selfish.

If you cannot afford the things you want to do without someone else's paying for you, let it be a reminder of your limitations, an encouragement to expand. Reality is creativity's best inspiration.

If you want to do something that badly, you'll do it. You'll make a plan or figure out a way. You can do it if you really want to.

And if you can't figure out a way to do what you want right now, then you have an even more valuable lesson to learn. Maybe you have to rethink how you live your life, what makes you happy, what you can and can't afford. Maybe your work needs to be more fulfilling so you don't feel you need to reward yourself for suffering at a boring job.

A happy life is scaled to your reality, not your fantasy.

A wealthy person can have anything he or she wants—but not everything.

A rich person needs nothing.

A poor person feels in debt to the entire world.

❧

I need nothing from others but understanding.
I give what I need to myself.
Whoever loves me loves me.
Who does not does not.

Make Your Life Better

❧

I t's entirely up to you.
Who else would know what you want or need but you?

If you are waiting for something to happen or someone to love you to make your life better, you'd better be sitting in a comfortable chair.

No one is coming.

And that's a good thing because the person who does come along and promises to make your life better is probably going to make it miserable as well.

If anything is going to get better, it will because you did something about it. So don't expect anything else.

They go hand in hand, disappointment and unrealistic expectations.

You were put in the center of your

life to take charge of it. Other people are just casual observers. They hardly notice when you do something good. They applaud in the wrong places anyhow, the places their interests lie. Their negative comments also have more to do with themselves than you. So praise is never going to be enough to make your life better, and criticism has limited value.

Shape your life to follow your instincts, your inclinations, and your preferences.

Make your life better, and *you* be the judge of what better means.

You have to live it, you might as well love it.

❧

I love my life.
I love the way I love it.
I intend the best for me.

Stay Out of Debt

More easily said than done.
All merchants give credit and ease you into debt with a smile. Our economic growth depends on your spending more money than you earn. You're encouraged to live for the moment, pay from the future, and regret the past.

If you borrow from your future, you limit your growth and fill the present with worry. When you're in debt you lament the past but seldom learn from it.

Borrow from your friends and you lose them.

Borrow from your parents and you stay a child.

You cannot create a happy life with a credit card. The more you borrow, the more unhappy you'll be.

Consider all the reasons you give why borrowing is a good idea and how you'll be able to repay in the future. You could be completely wrong, you know.

Don't be discouraged by this. But if you do feel discouraged, it probably has more to do with your being in debt than anything you've just read.

By the way, could someone as bright and as hardworking as you have made such incorrect decisions about money?

You've tried to buy happiness. Maybe not at the moment that you took the expensive loan or got a second mortgage, but all the way up till then. The big loan was just the tip of the iceberg of your desperation.

When are you going to learn?

❧

I accept where I am and how I got here.

Forgive

❧

I t's time. What is the point of keeping your hurt alive?

To justify your anger and make you feel better about plotting your revenge? Not a good place to live, in a mind that is filled with hate, and you are frozen in hatred when you don't forgive.

You don't want to forgive? You probably have good reasons, a long list of good reasons. Without arguing with the fact that you were hurt, why is it that you are the one who is still suffering?

Forgiving is the next step and the last step.

Forgiving is letting go of your hurt.

If you are holding onto your pain because you want to show the person who hurt you how much damage he or she caused you, or if you act in a self-defeating way, always courting failure, allowing success to slip through your life, displaying your hurt by playing the role of a damaged person, perhaps you are making a big mistake.

If the person who hurt you could be influenced by your suffering to feel guilt and remorse and make amends to you, he or she would most likely be the kind of person who never would have hurt you in the first place.

Life always gets complicated when you conceal your hurt and wait for people to come to you and apologize. Your withheld hurt turns into anger and makes you victimize yourself.

If you expect others to make repairs, you're always disappointed.

You need to forgive as much as you deserve to be forgiven.

You need to forgive if ever you are
to love again.

❧

I release my hurt.
I allow the past to fade.
I am here.
My pain is gone.

Take
Responsibility

❧

If things turn out badly, you'll probably be blamed, so take responsibility now and make events go the way you want.

When you don't take responsibility, you give up control to others. Others never have your real interests at heart because they really don't know you. And if they did, why should they do for you what you won't do for yourself? Make your interests known to yourself and take action.

Take responsibility for everything that you have done and for everything you have avoided doing. It's the first step toward being free.

The greatest gift you can give children is to let them take responsibility for themselves.

Whenever you take responsibility for other people, you limit their growth. They may be grateful initially, but the more responsibility you take, the more they will resent you.

Take responsibility for knowing how you feel, what you need, and what you want. Unless you do, *yes* and *no* are meaningless words.

Take responsibility for everything that has happened to you, that shaped you, whether you caused it or not.

You're responsible for suffering.

You're responsible for living happily ever after.

The responsibility that you accept ceases to be a burden.

You may not be responsible for what happened to you, but you are re-

sponsible for what you feel about it and
how you reacted toward it.

❧

I am responsible for everything in my
life.
I am responsible for what I was.
I am responsible for what I will
become.

When a Dark
Memory Returns

❧

D on't fight it.
    Permit the intrusion without
regret.

Let the memory or old feeling have
its way with you.

The sadness of a lost love, a rebuke
or betrayal, or a hurt that cut deeply
left you wounded. It returns, takes your
breath away, gives you pause.

Measure the depth of the hurt, but
from the safe distance time provides.

Know that because the hurt is past,
the resentment will cool.

Don't push the painful feeling or
memory away.

If you let it through without resist-
ing it, it will pass.

Push it away and it will build, seeking the expression it needs to relieve the old pressure.

That is the way of old pain, pressing to the surface till it fades. Old pain comes in waves.

How can you stop a wave?

Ride the reappearance of your old emotions, but don't try to hold them back. You'll use up your energy, lose faith in yourself, doubt your strength and wholeness, and ruin your day.

Let the old hurt pass, acknowledging all that it means, and in a moment it will be gone. The hurt is diminished, and so is the likelihood of return.

The moment is returned to you.

❧

I allow my memories to return and
have their way.
I let the past replay but do not live in
it.
I let old feelings flow through me on
their way to peace.
I accept all that I was, all that has
been.
I accept all of it—all of me.

Accept Your Death

❧

If you don't accept your death, what meaning can your life have?

Don't be put off by the morbidity of this.

You are mortal, and, being precious, you have a problem. You need to take care of yourself without becoming obsessed with your health, to be safe and still take the right risks.

Death should come as a friend at the end of your days when you're weary and the road impassable, not because you took reckless chances to test your mortality. If you try to deny death, you end up losing your life.

Death is not an option. It is imposed upon us. Just like life.

The best preparation for dying is finding yourself.

It doesn't matter where you are on the road when death comes but that you are on the right road, making the right journey, to a destination you chose.

Your life is your adventure; your death, just another reminder. Acknowledging your end imparts urgency to making the right beginning.

Who are you?

Why are you here?

Where are you going?

What will you leave behind?

You live deliberately by being honest in each moment, solving your problems as life presents them to you, by feeling your pain openly, surrendering to joy, giving in love, and by expecting nothing.

In the end they are going to kill you. Accept this.

Your life is your only reward. Live it so that it is worth dying for.

❧

**I live every moment.
I begin my life anew each day.**

Don't Be Lazy

◆

No one really wants to work, especially when the work is someone else's and moves you toward a goal that has nothing to do with what your life is about.

It's easy to feel lazy when you don't find any purpose in what you're doing.

Money soon loses its power to motivate you. Money is like that. Pursuing it makes you crazy.

Even if you grab the brass ring on the merry-go-round, you can sometimes feel pretty stupid that, after winning a meaningless symbol, you are still going around in circles, still pleasing others.

What can anything mean, really mean, that is not of yourself?

You're never lazy when you do

what you love, although sometimes you're just afraid and push the work you love away. You're only afraid of the right work because you don't want to discover unpleasant truths about yourself. The right work tells on you.

It can reveal that you are not as competent as you would like to be.

Or not as talented, and that you are really going to have to work at your success.

Or not as special, and that you have nothing very earth-shattering to say.

Or not as original, and that you have a lot of growing to do.

Join the club. If you risk doing what you are supposed to do, you may make the sad discovery that you are not as good as you had hoped, but you also may find that you are not as bad as you had feared.

Your life started a long time ago.
Are you on the right road? Are you
doing what you want to be doing?

Now what is all this laziness about?

❧

**I seek my life's work, my being and
purpose.
I am not afraid to discover my worth,
for I already love myself.**

Believe in Yourself

O K, have it your way, don't believe
in yourself.

If you don't believe in yourself, you
are obligated to believe in whoever will
take care of you.

Or go and believe in yourself so
completely that you don't admit any
weaknesses or mistakes. Some people
need to believe in themselves 100 percent just to believe in themselves at all.
As a matter of fact, having to believe in
yourself 100 percent is probably the
same as not believing in yourself at all.

You need to believe in yourself to
perform, to give, to accept, to love, to
be open. Your belief in yourself is your
most important strength.

Your belief in yourself is the most
important endorsement you'll ever get.

If everyone believes in you but you, you'll never take the risk to find your purpose, to accomplish your work, or to find real love.

Others' belief in you is important, but only to remind you to believe in yourself, for others' belief means nothing unless *you* believe.

You've always been alone in this, even though you can look back to earlier times when people once stood by you, praised you, urged you on to victory. Still, it was your belief that carried the day.

It feels harder to believe in yourself when no one else does, but your belief is always your invention, your fantasy of your best, your acceptance, your dream. You can still create that belief. You always did. You'll always need to.

You're your own best witness to your experience. And to that secret, evolving self that can someday change the world, you are usually the only witness.

The people who do it believe in themselves against all odds.

So believe in your passion.

Believe in your gift.

Believe in your purpose.

Even when you don't.

❧

I believe in me.
I believe in my gift.

You Deserve

❧

Y ou deserve the best.
   It's true.

You deserve, even if you don't think you are deserving.

You don't think you deserve to be treated badly? Well, it's true. You don't deserve to be treated badly.

But the sad truth is that you deserve just what you accept.

If you don't like what is happening to you, it is up to you to say something and do something about it.

Don't complain. You deserve exactly what you tolerate.

Don't expect others to change.

You deserve the best.

You settle for less only because you don't believe you deserve.

You're going to have to take a leap

of faith and believe that you're deserving. Your belief that you are deserving allows people to give to you and opens the world to your giving.

You deserve to give of your best as well as to receive the best. The world deserves to hear from you. As a matter of fact, the world *needs* to hear from you.

Maybe the reason you don't feel deserving is that you aren't giving enough of what you were put here to give.

❧

I deserve all the good I can imagine, all the joy I can carry, the company of friends, the love of myself.
All the good.
I deserve it.

Celebrate

That you are alive.

That you won.

That although you were beaten, you are still here.

That you feel.

That a hummingbird visited you.

That the breeze carried the perfume of spring.

That the car started and the brakes held.

That the sunset was mauve and golden umber.

That the rose broke through at last and bloomed.

That you cried.

That you were remembered.

That you remember.

That the wind carried a message of hope.

That you love.

That you once loved.

That all music and art were in-tended just for you.

That you were right.

That you forgave.

That it rained and the rain forgave all of us.

That you are human, after all.

I celebrate my completeness,
incomplete as I am.
I celebrate my laughter breaking
through my tears.
I celebrate now.
I celebrate being.

Don't Argue

It's pointless.

Other people have already made up their minds.

What do you hope to accomplish by shouting your opinions?

To change people's perception of you?

You can't convince other people that you are wonderful. You can try, of course, but you'll only raise questions about your self-doubt.

If you think you have changed others' minds by yelling at them, you are just fooling yourself. You have only bullied them.

Intimidation breeds resentment, not respect.

Besides, you can't make anyone like you.

And trying to win someone's love by arguing is ridiculous if not abusive. Arguments of love generally become abusive. When you try to persuade someone to love you, you only invite the other person to use you, and you also name the price you'll pay to be abused.

When you argue with someone you love, you always end up feeling guilty and needy at the same time, trying to convince yourself that the person you hurt deserved it. Worse, in that state you both want the other's affection but are unable either to admit that you do or to accept it. Your guilt makes you feel pretty unlovable.

When you argue, you never resolve anything. You only push yourself to the limit of your frustration. The other person goes to the same point. Neither of you are being your best, and both of you get worse by the minute.

Scream at the wind if you must. At least you won't be disappointed when your efforts come to nothing.

And you won't feel guilty for being out of control.

❧

I let others be themselves.
I allow room for disagreement.
I savor the difference between myself and others and do not contest it.
My victory is in being me.

Listen

❧

S ome wonderful advice for you:
Just listen.

Listen. When other people are talking, let them express their thoughts, their opinions, and their feelings, especially their feelings. Don't just let them talk; listen to what they are saying. Pay attention. Try to understand.

Listen. You don't have to agree. As a matter of fact, whether you agree or not should be beside the point. Don't express your opinions or feelings while someone else is expressing his or hers. Do you have a problem with that? Do you feel you need to express your opinion, that you must make your feelings known? When others are speaking, you won't be heard anyway, and you'll just lose points for trying.

Listen without waiting for an opportunity to give your side, or pounce on the other person, or correct his or her mistakes. The other person's reasoning and information is surely full of mistakes and distortions. So what? So is yours.

Listen in sincere silence. It won't kill you. You don't need to prove your point. Just listen. Everyone thinks a good listener is smart.

Listen. You don't need to persuade the other person, just understand. If you don't, ask, "Could you explain that?" or "What do you really mean?" But don't give your opinion while the other person is talking. Just let him or her talk.

The good listener hears the unspoken thought. Listen for it. When the other person is finished, mention that inner thought. The other person will know you heard and understood.

Then the situation will become quiet because the other person will be listening to your hearing. All the pressure will fade and you can get on with life.

Listen. There is nothing quite like being heard.

🐦

I listen to the space between the words others speak.
I live in the silence where knowing dwells.
I make room for life by creating stillness.

Be Gracious

✦

You don't have to measure the world by a perfect standard. It's boring and demoralizing because everyone will fail your test.

When someone tells you you did a good job, just say "thank you." Don't point out how you failed to reach your goals. Or when someone tells you they like your clothes or your performance, don't put yourself down. That's not humble.

Putting yourself down sets you up as superior. It sounds a lot like you are just fishing for compliments. You are, by the way. But more important, you're putting the other person down, in effect saying "what could you possibly know?" You're belittling the other person's opinion. Not nice. Not at all gracious.

Be gracious in accepting thanks and appreciation.

Be gracious in acknowledging your debt to others. You didn't invent the wheel, and no matter how much you think your work is worth, you had plenty of help on the way to your success, even from those you think stood in your way. Be especially gracious to them.

Be gracious in forgiving debts.

Be gracious for favors that others do for you, particularly when the situation that inspired their generosity revealed your weakness.

Be gracious when someone remembers you.

Be gracious forgiving common oversights. Others are busy and overwhelmed. So someone forgot. Why make such a big deal out of it? Do you need reassurance that much?

When you're gracious, other people become gracious, remember their manners, put things in perspective, apologize, and make friends.

All it takes is one person being gracious about a difficult situation to make it better.

❧

I realize that few things really matter
that much.
I accept that everything is on time.
It is only desperation and anxiety that
make them seem late.
I accept that where I am is right,
and that where other people are is
right for them.

Take the Time to Be Beautiful

❧

It only takes a moment longer to do it right.

When you rush, you lose your place in your mind, your balance totters, your purpose dissipates.

Take time to see the beauty around you.

Take time to see the order, the existing plan, the architecture of the place.

Take time to see the balance, the imbalance, the light, the shade, the full places about to be emptied, the empty places about to be filled.

Take time to see the difference, the contrast, the supporters, and the antagonists.

Take time to see how you fit in.

Take time to find the right path,

the course of passion, and the highest good.

Take time to find your place, and know before you do that it is always changing. Know that you have to be changing to fit in harmoniously.

Take time to know the intent of others, to understand the direction of the wind, the ebb of tides, and the emerging cloud faces.

Take time to see beauty.

Take time to know your response.

Take time to be beautiful.

The beauty that escapes you leaves a hungry soul behind.

I appreciate the natural goodness of
the human spirit.
I realize how easily flowers fade.
I accept that life is fleeting, and know
how all of this beauty can slip away if
I do not take the time to notice.

L i f e

&

The purpose of life is to discover your gift.

The work of life is to develop it.

The meaning of life is to give your gift away.

&

I know I have a purpose.
I believe in my gift.
I am here to give.
When I am in doubt, I give more.

The Secret of Life

The secret of life is that there is no secret of life.
It's all hard work.

**I welcome each day to continue my
giving.
I give of myself until I am full, and
then I give the rest.**

Take a Risk

Unless you do, it's not going to happen.

The dream, the plan, the vindication by triumph, the love that heals, the balmy climate where you can live languidly, the new body you want to build, the education, the career, the home, the travel, the gain, and all the glory.

All that you want, all that you cherish depends on you taking a risk.

Everything involves a risk. *Everything!*

Nothing in this world is static, so you have to risk all the time.

You risk to grow. You grow to stay young, to have hope, to believe in the world as you create it.

Risking isn't easy. If it were, it wouldn't be a risk.

What do you risk?

You always risk losing something you care about when you risk, because a risk isn't a step. A risk is a leap.

What could you lose?

Your belief that you are safe? You're only safe if you keep on risking.

Your belief that you are happy? You are only happy if you are growing.

Your belief that your work is done? If you are alive, your work is always just beginning.

You need to risk to adapt, to discover, to know, to learn, to give up, to let go, to see fully, to accept the world and what it bestows.

You need to risk to find yourself.

You need to risk to live.

❧

I can.
I know I want to . . .
I can.
I know I have to . . .
I can.
Yes!
I can.

Live Your Own Life

❧

You already know you have to.
Living your life for other people is just not fulfilling.

Be clear about this. The people whose lives benefit others most follow their own dream. Mother Teresa doesn't do what she does because she feels she should. She wants to. Her giving is special because it is from her heart, not to please someone else. The same was true for Mozart, Einstein, and van Gogh.

There is a big difference between *should* and *want to*.

Live your life doing what you want to do.

If you do what you feel you must do, your obligation should be to yourself. Saying, "I have to follow my dream," "I need to be true to myself," or "I've got to complete my life's work" makes sense. Following inner desires leads you to be happy as yourself. You continue to grow and become your best.

When, just to please others, you feel obligated to do things or become something that has nothing to do with your dream, you waste your time. And if you waste enough of your time, you waste your life. You end up resenting the very people you are obligated to, the same people you're trying to please.

No appreciation can ever be worth your sacrifice when you have sacrificed yourself.

Whether they are your parents, your spouse, or your children, after a while others start to expect that you will always do for them. And when you do for others, they do not learn to do for themselves and so you rob them of their self-esteem.

Change and you may discover that others resent you, withhold their love, pressure you to give in. They'll probably think you're being unfair, but how can you be fair to yourself if you don't do what is right for you?

Your life should fulfill your needs and desires and allow you to make your mark and follow your own direction.

That's why you were put here, to find your gift and give it.

That's your job.

That's your destiny.

You create it by being true to yourself.

Of course when you do live your own life, you will still have obligations that do not seem to support your dreams, such as housekeeping, errands, and paying taxes, but at least you will be doing your own chores. You probably will have to keep your day job in order to support yourself. It comes with being responsible, but the satisfaction of finally living your own life will encourage you and give you the energy to succeed.

None of this is meant to suggest that you shouldn't be nice to others. It means that you should do something besides just being nice to other people.

My life is the gift; my talent, the vehicle; my moment, now.

Tell the Truth

❧

Most of your problems come from not telling the truth.

The lies you tell, even to spare other people's feelings, always come back to haunt you.

If you simply tell people what you mean you would be better off, a lot happier, not trapped in some awkward social situation. Others will know where they stand and will be more honest with you.

They won't expect you to be what you're not. They won't need to test you to discover your intentions. You won't have to make excuses for not doing things you didn't want to do or explain why you prefer to do what you like to do. They'll know.

Telling the truth and being your

own person are closely linked. A strong person says what he or she means. A weak person lies to please others. A strong person lets the truth be other people's problem. A weak person holds the truth inside and complains about being treated unfairly.

What if telling the truth hurts other people's feelings? You're not supposed to tell people that they look fat, or are stupid or ugly. That's just being rude.

Tell the truth about what you feel, want, and like and mean what you say. If others get hurt by your truth, they'll have to deal with it. Others may not like what you say, but they'll respect you for being honest and they'll survive better than if you lie to them.

If you lie to please people, they won't really believe you. They'll be suspicious and suffer with every inconsistency they find in your story. You'll be called on to update alibis and others will undermine you and try to trap you. People hate being lied to, because lying takes away their free choice and their ability to defend themselves.

Tell the truth. It only hurts once. Lies hurt everyone all the time.

🐦

I know the truth by speaking the truth.
I learn the truth by listening.
The truth I tell becomes me.

The Truth

❧

L ive your life so that the truth is
 your friend.

The truth is the beginning of freedom.

The truth *is* freedom.

The truth is its own explanation.

One truth admits all others.

The truth is within you.

Don't fight it. Admitting the truth
only hurts when it should.

It only takes one small truth to
pierce your false illusions, and yet one
truth can set your whole life straight.

The truth is the cure for confusion.

Only being loyal to truth will com-
fort you.

Being able to hear the truth is being able to understand the mysteries of
your life and connect them.

People will only tell you the truth that you are able to hear. And so you can only have others' love if you can hear all of their truth.

If love is anything, love is the truth.

Where the truth is most easily expressed, stress is lowest.

Courage comes when you seek the truth.

Healing begins when you accept it.

Tell the truth so you're not in pain and can love the world again.

❧

I want to know what is so.
I want to see what is.
I want to be what I am.

Mind Your Own
Business

❧

People who stick their noses in other people's business don't have much going on in their own lives.

It's not your business to know who is having an affair, a nervous breakdown, going bankrupt, or getting divorced.

Insecure people are always looking at what other people are doing. They become so afraid someone is about to overtake them that they stop concentrating on their own goals.

Unless you're directly involved, what other people are doing or thinking isn't your business.

But in case you want to know, others, like you, are sifting through confusing facts, trying to sort truth from distortion and figure out what to do next. Other people feel lost much of the time and worry, trying to cover their mistakes.

If you could know what others were thinking and react to it, your life would become crazy. Believe this.

It's not your business to figure out if other people are doing better or worse than you. Besides, how can you really tell what you are comparing yourself with?

What good is it to pride yourself on being more productive than a loafer or better than some incompetent braggart?

Worse, you begin to doubt yourself when you believe others are ahead of you, and if you believe you are ahead of others you may become complacent and lose your momentum.

If you do mind other people's business, sooner or later you're going to act on your curiosity and say or do something intrusive that you're bound to regret.

And while you are minding other people's business, who's minding yours?

❧

I am moving forward.
What happens on the side is not my concern.
I look away from my goals only because I forget to believe.
I continue to look ahead.
I believe in me.

An Open Heart Is the Best Teacher

❧

Education doesn't make you happy. Success doesn't make you kind.

Poverty doesn't make you wise.

Riches don't make you full.

Experience doesn't make you smart.

But love can teach you everything.

❧

I expect nothing but to be.
I desire nothing but to learn.
I am nothing, but am becoming
everything.

Finding Your Way

Y ou are the artist creating your life.
You are a work in progress.

Your search is also your goal.

Your identity will be revealed through your quest of that goal.

Your work is always to find your work.

Your belief in yourself becomes your life.

Act on what you believe is right and the rest will take care of itself.

Find something to give to the world and only settle for things that make sense to you.

Don't try to make all things possible. Stay with one goal and it will teach you everything.

You are always living the life you create.

If your life doesn't feel right, create
something better.

🍂

My work is the way.
My love is the way.
My past is the way.
This moment is the way.
I am the way.

Don't Give Up

❧

L et the positive forces in your life take over.

You have to risk rejection to get what you want.

You have to risk failure to find success.

Learn to cherish, not lament.

Find the ally, not the enemy.

Remember your long-term goals during your short-term problems.

Instead of imagining negative things that fill you with terror, invent positive things that fill you with purpose.

Don't give up, give more.

❧

I yield to the good.
I come from strength.
I give my best.

Follow Your Heart

❧

Follow your heart and have the courage to dream, for what you dream becomes your life.

What dream should you dream?

The first answer your heart speaks is the truest.

When you tell that truth to yourself, it becomes apparent to the world.

Follow what you love.

That is always the right direction.

When your intention is clear, the path opens up.

Find that course.

Stay on it.

Believe in yourself.

When you lose your direction, look inside to find it again.

It will always be in the same place.

❧

**I open my heart and hear myself
speaking the truth. I open my heart
and see myself finding my way.**

Be Yourself

You are the unchanging you.

   You are the same you that you were when you were a child and the same you that you will be on your last day.

   And yet you can only be your best as you are now, not as you used to be, not as you will be in twenty years.

   You can only be your best as yourself, not in imitation of someone else, not by following someone else's standards, only by fulfilling your own.

   Be yourself, not what other people want or need you to be.

   Wherever you can be yourself is the place you are supposed to be. You cannot be your best where you do not feel like yourself.

The person you should be with is the person in whose presence you feel most like yourself, most like your best.

When you have to give up part of yourself to be with another person, you always miss the part that you sacrificed in order to be together, and you hold the other person hostage for the part of yourself you miss.

When you are lonely it is always for that missing part of yourself.

Your work should be about you. It should mirror your best and capture your desire. You should be able to find yourself by losing yourself in your work.

When you are bored, you are not living your own life.

You don't have to try, you just have to be.

Be yourself where you are right now.

Every part of your life should tell
your life story, for if you own yourself
fully, you possess the world.

❧

**I seek myself in everything I do.
I find myself.
I dream my dream wherever I go.
I become myself.**

Come from Love

❧

Coming from love is being open, truthful, and simple.

When you come from love, you initiate your actions from the belief that you are deserving and that other people are good.

It makes perfect sense.

Look for trouble and you'll find it.

Ask what's wrong and people will tell you.

The good can be fleeting and become lost behind suspicion and self-doubt. So discover what is right and bring it out in others.

Don't worry. What is wrong and problematic will still be there to work on when you return to it later.

When you come from love, you do not play the fool or become a doormat, for coming from love means first of all that you love yourself. When you do it's harder for others to take advantage of you.

When you come from love, you're the most open. Deception seems obvious to you and you feel less inhibited about speaking out.

When you come from love, you're simply being your best.

When you come from love, you create love around you.

When you come from love, you live in a loving world.

I find love when I look within. . . .
I create love all around me.
I see the signs of love
everywhere I look. . . .
I remember I am lovable.

Don't Take It Personally

🐾

People are selfish. They're wrapped up in their own world. They don't notice your suffering or celebrate your success.

Don't take it personally.

Disinterest seems to be the way of the world. This is neither wrong nor right, neither good nor bad. It simply is the way it is.

Think how it would be if people did notice every time you did something wrong. They'd point it out to you. They'd confuse you with suggestions. They'd anger you with their intrusions. It would be harder to make corrections and move on.

Don't take it personally when a stranger gets angry at you; assume that it has nothing to do with you. He'd been holding in his feelings a long time before you came into his life.

Don't take it personally when the IRS comes calling, when your neighbor complains about your dog, when your car breaks down right after you had it fixed, or when the computer fails and important data are lost.

The negativity that you choose to react to is only a sounding board for what you feel inside. These same events would have happened whether you were there or not. If you didn't feel bad about yourself, you never would have taken the events of the world so personally.

The outside world has nothing to do with you.

The world is within you—all the caring, all the sublime inspiration, all the doubt.

The way you react to the world only reflects how you feel about yourself.

❧

**I remember that I am the world within.
The outside world does not concern me.
My world is filled with me.**

Seek the Good
in Others

❧

This is not about being a do-gooder. It's about being smart, efficient, and productive.

It's about making your life easy.

When you look for the good in others, they show it to you.

When you appreciate their worth, others find it easy to be their best.

When you accept others, they don't fear rejection. They show their strengths instead of concealing their weaknesses. They act confident instead of afraid.

Other people want someone to notice that they are good and valuable. They want to belong and to be thought of as special.

They need someone to believe in them.

Looking for the good is that belief.

Look for the good in the other person, especially when he or she has been troublesome, did wrong, or is on probation. Don't ignore his or her problems, but continue to encourage the good.

Anyone who doubts can find failings.

Finding the good takes belief.

When you bring out the good in someone you often discover a powerful ally, a loyal worker, a true friend.

The search for the good is its own reward.

The discovery of that good is never forgotten.

When you look for the good in others, you often discover your own best

and find another reason to believe in
yourself.

I look for the gift others have to give.
I remind others of their worth.
I rejoice in all the good I discover.

Don't Complain

❧

No one wants to hear it. When you complain, you just anger others.

Complaining is always hurtful because it adds stress and pressure to an already problematic situation.

Others have a gut reaction to your complaining. It grates on their nerves. They want to shut you off and push you away.

Complainers are like childish passengers, continually whining, "Are we there yet?" They aggravate others by increasing stress and frustration and by creating distracting resentment that interferes with productivity.

It's no wonder that complaining makes you seem inadequate and damages your credibility.

People complain most about what they don't want to do or feel they can't do for themselves. So complaining also shows that you are not in charge and reveals your lack of patience and inability to act for yourself.

Complaining creates the wrong atmosphere for making a change.

It's better to ask a question couched in friendly and helpful terms such as, "Is there any way I can help?" Every complaint can be rephrased in this way.

If you complain when someone asks you to do something, it spoils the effect of doing what you've been asked.

When you complain, you are really protesting against your own powerlessness and helplessness.

The weaknesses you can't face in yourself are what you complain about most in others.

❧

I take responsibility for my life.
I have the power to make things
better.
I always have a choice.

Your Attitude

&

Your attitude shapes your world. When you intimidate others, you live in a fearful world.

When you are sad, you bring out the hopelessness in others.

When you express support, you live in others' affection.

When you act like a child, you evoke a parental attitude. When you act like a parent, you inspire both rebellion and helplessness.

When you act dependent, you invite others to abuse you. They resent you for smothering them.

When you act controlling, you lead people to use you. They think you have it coming for treating them unfairly.

When you act competitively, others want to beat you for putting them down.

Your attitude creates obstacles that you have to overcome and all your lucky breaks. No one wants to help a braggart, and everyone wants to repay the person who makes him or her feel good.

The person who makes you feel good is free, has no need to control or own you, can admire your achievements without envy, and can be giving without expecting anything in return.

Your pattern of choices becomes your attitude. When you choose to hold in feelings, you become bitter. When you are expressive, you become free.

Being free is letting others be free. In this world you get what you give.

❧

Because I am free to be myself, I allow others to be free and I can see the world as it is.

Admit That You're Human

●

I t's time for a reality check.

You're only human and you make mistakes.

You also hurt others.

Although it is hard to admit, you hurt others intentionally, and you hurt them the most when you deny that you did it.

Your parents weren't perfect. They weren't always wise, giving, and understanding.

Your parents weren't complete monsters or total idiots either. They did the best they could as they saw that best from their viewpoint.

Just like you.

In your most recent disagreement you were partly wrong, even if you don't want to admit it.

And the last time someone thought you were brilliant, little did they know.

You can be petty when you are insecure, totally withholding when you doubt yourself, and hateful, unsupportive, and vengeful when you feel desperate.

You are also capable of being brave, giving, loving, understanding, and compassionate.

Whatever you are, just admit it.

Admit your humanness. It's always a sign of strength.

Admit your humanness and give others something to love.

❧

I am just a person.
I aspire to the stars.
If I succeed, I am still just a person.
If I aspire, I cannot fail.

Correct Your Lies

❧

Most of the difficulties you're struggling with could have been avoided by simply telling the truth.

It's hard to correct a lie, especially when you've been denying it.

The longer you deny a lie, the more you believe it.

When you are forced to believe in a lie, you're no longer free.

When you lie, your best intentions lack all conviction.

A lie takes energy to maintain, generates anxiety over being discovered, and wastes time covering itself up.

The truth makes its own case. The truth may be hard at first, but it's easiest in the long run.

You need to accept that, like everyone else, you sometimes take liberties with the truth.

You slant facts to make yourself appear right, especially when you think you're wrong.

You hide your faults and conceal your errors.

You exaggerate numbers to impress people, distort events to save face, and minimize hurts to protect yourself.

When you hear yourself telling a lie, correct it on the spot.

Simply say, "I misspoke," and add, "What I really meant to say was . . . ," completing the thought, telling the truth.

If you do so quickly and matter-of-factly, no one will even notice.

If you want, you can explain the disappointment your misstatement was about to obscure, since all distortion conceals disappointment. Perhaps you can even share the dream that still eludes you.

Your openness in correcting your lies disarms others, declares your honesty, and wins you friends.

🐑

I do not expect to be perfect.
I learn from everything and everyone.
Openly and freely I admit my
mistakes.
Without shame I correct them.

Express Your Hurt

❧

The surest way to become unhappy is to keep your hurt inside.

If there is a secret to mental health, this is it: tell the people who hurt you that they hurt you when they hurt you.

Hurt is the pain of the moment. Hurt is happening right now. Its cause is right in front of you. Hurt speaks for itself, motivating you to limit your pain.

Anxiety is pain in the future. It may happen, and then again, it may not. Anxiety inspires you to get out of the way of danger.

Withheld hurt turns into anger. Anger helps you express your hurt by energizing you to protect yourself.

When you hold in hurt, you redirect your anger at yourself. Such inward anger is called guilt. It serves no positive purpose. It only makes you think of getting even, fills your head with bad thoughts, and erodes your self-confidence as you begin to doubt your goodness.

Obviously the only anger that makes sense is still attached to the hurt that caused it.

You need to learn to express your hurt as it happens.

Telling someone how he or she hurt you can be risky, because the person who hurt you is probably someone you care about.

What if the other person calls you "oversensitive" or tells you that your hurt is unimportant and doesn't take your feelings seriously?

If the other person doesn't care about your feelings, he or she doesn't care about you. The sooner you know this, the better. Why waste more time?

What if the other person says he or she hurt you out of anger because of being hurt by you? It's a good time to discover the truth, clear the air, and become friends again.

What if the other person can't remember hurting you or simply denies that the hurtful event ever took place?

He or she may be telling the truth, because most people do not hurt others intentionally. When you are silent it is sometimes hard for others to recognize that you've been hurt.

Expressing your hurt sometimes puts your love or friendship on the line. It always tests your love for yourself.

It is always the right thing to do in any relationship that you value.

Express your hurt as simply and as directly as possible when you first notice it.

Tell the other person how you were hurt. You can mention that you are angry, but don't display the anger or attack. That will only hurt the other person, who won't be able to listen, making matters worse.

Whatever you do, don't allow your hurt to age.

If you cannot express your hurt to another person, you cannot express your love, for old anger blocks positive feelings.

If you value your love, you need to express your hurt.

Holding in hurt is the way that love dies.

❧

I show my hurt when I am hurt so I can feel love the rest of the time.

Be Open

To be open is to be willing to see and be seen.

Openness is based on self-acceptance and a desire to grow.

Openness and freedom are linked. Only the open are free.

Only the free are open.

Love only flourishes in openness.

It is hate and suffering that prosper in secret.

The feelings you hold in take over your life.

Open your heart. If you lock too many feelings away, you lose yourself.

The painful truth told now is better than an unhappy life lived in silence. Tell it.

The feelings you don't admit take

over your life and imprison you. Admit them.

There are no mysteries to life when you are open.

Being open is living your best life.

When you're open, you become free to leave the mark you're supposed to.

When you are open, all the answers are knowable.

🐘

**I am open to the mysteries of life,
and being open, I find none.
I am open to the pain of life,
and being open, I find pleasure.**

Secrets

❧

You are as burdened as the secrets you keep.

When you keep a secret from someone else, you are robbing that person of his or her free will to act and do what is best.

When the secret is known, its keeping will be the issue. "Why so long?" "Why didn't you trust me?" "Why didn't you believe in me?"

You may be forgiven for the secret you kept, but the hurt for keeping it will fester.

A secret is a cousin to a lie.

When you exclude people from the truth they need to know to protect themselves, you only make them weaker.

When you keep a secret to allow

another person to avoid his or her own destiny, you become a force against that person.

When you keep a secret, you close down part of yourself.

When someone asks you to keep a secret, he or she burdens your heart and asks you to suffer too.

Most secrets you don't want to know.

You never thank someone for telling you a secret.

When you are told a secret, you are robbed of your spontaneous reaction to another person.

Since secrets are hidden, some part of the secret is also false, but since the secret is silent you can never inquire what part of it is real.

A life of secrets is a kind of hell.

Where secrets exist, love perishes.

☙

I have no secrets.
I have nothing to hide.
Even if I discover the worst about me,
the discovery will be a new strength.

Grow Up

❧

These may sound like harsh words. You've probably heard them before, spoken in anger when you did something wrong or something that other people didn't like.

"Grow up and take responsibility."

"Grow up and pay your own way."

"Grow up and make your own decisions."

"Grow up and stop bothering me."

No one wants to pay taxes, go to work, face the inevitable, mourn the impossible, compromise unrealistic dreams, or accept their limitations, but this is the way of life.

We all want to play. We all have to work.

The happiest people maintain their playfulness in their work, because their work is an extension of their best.

You can do it too.

If you do not find play in your work, you may appear grown up and serious to others, but you have just grown old.

To find play in your work, you have to find yourself.

You have to grow up to take responsibility for believing in yourself, for believing that you have something special to give.

Once you believe, you will start taking your specialness seriously. That's being grown up, especially if your work feels like play all the time.

Nothing is more serious or grown up than people who have found themselves.

It's time to grow up and start playing your own game.

I can be everything to myself.

Claim Your
Freedom

❧

Freedom is not a destination. It's a journey.

You need to be free to choose the right road for yourself. The right road is the one that leads to your best.

All that matters is that you end up a free person—free to decide where you want to go and how you intend to get there.

The method is simple: act freely and freedom will be yours.

Because being free is being real, if you want to be free, you need to make friends with the truth.

No matter how clearly you can point to forces blocking you, the most important obstacles to your freedom are within.

You are the one who permits obstacles to block your path. While being stuck is frustrating, it also keeps you from risking, safe from failure and from discovering your weaknesses and shortcomings.

Your prison is always your choice.

To break free, you have to give up whatever security being bound offers.

You should be able to face the present without the emotions of the past intruding. In the end you're only as free as you are in your heart.

Your freedom lies just behind your forgiving.

When you free yourself, you also free the world.

❧

I am free.
I declare it.

Find Your Own
Path

❧

There are no rules for this, no courses you can take in school.

The teachers you meet along the way point out a direction, but it is their direction. You follow it because it seems strong to you in the time of your uncertainty.

If you are lucky, you become lost.

Losing your way is always a positive step once you get over the fear. Getting lost is proof you were mistaken and motivates you to make a correction.

No one goes as far astray as the person who makes a false decision early in life just to have a direction to follow.

Oh, how wonderful it would be if we were all so abundantly gifted in childhood that our talent cut its own path before us. But that doesn't happen very often.

Your education probably diluted your enthusiasm for what you love rather than encouraged it. Your parents probably supported education over your natural gifts. It's hard not to feel a little like a trained monkey today, educated to fill someone else's requirements while your own inner directives are not regarded seriously.

Since even a bright talent shines dimly in the beginning, at first it is hard to believe in yourself and your true direction. Should you try and then find your efforts less than you hoped, you may abandon your path for a more secure road. No one likes to fail.

You are your direction. All you have to do is harness your best intentions. Claim your own desire. Accept

your strengths and limitations and allow whatever gift you have to lead you.

Your gift first presents itself as a
love. Your talent holds your attention
and attracts you to details. All genius
lies in attention to details.

You can follow whatever road you
choose, but if the way you travel is not
your own, what difference does it make
that you followed it?

❧

This is my journey.
This is my life.
I create the road as I walk.

Make Your Own
Mistakes

❧

Don't be afraid to make mistakes. You learn only from your mistakes.

Your successes don't teach you very much. Life is always changing. Your success could have been luck. You're sure to fail if you only try to imitate old successes and never risk enough to make mistakes.

Your biggest successes evolve through your failures.

You can learn from the mistakes of others, but you only grow through making your own.

Your mistakes point out your flaws, teach you to have confidence in your strengths and have a healthy respect for your humanness.

Your mistakes make you accessible to yourself. It is easier to review your life and make a powerful change during a mistake than it is during a success. Success lures you into believing you are better than you are.

While making a mistake can be deflating, it also reconnects you to your promise to yourself. You want the people you love most when they leave you. You want the work situation most when you have lost it.

When you are disappointed, your goals seem clearer.

Make your own mistakes on the road to your own goals.

Loosen up, take a chance, run the risk of growing again.

The mistake you make could just be the new beginning you've been looking for.

🐌

I am always ready to risk.
I am always ready to learn.
I am always ready to test my strength,
and so I put worry aside and just live.

Say No

❧

If you don't want to do something, say no.

Is that difficult for you?

The ease you have in saying no is a good measure of your freedom and potential for happiness.

Think about it. Why should you have a problem indicating you don't want to do what you don't want to do? Are you afraid of hurting someone, causing a scene, testing another person's affections?

When you say yes instead of no you only set the other person up to expect you to continue saying yes. Then when you finally do risk saying no you'll really disappoint the other person, sound like you don't know your own mind, and create an opening for dispute.

You can say no. Practice in front of a mirror, but try not to make too much of this. It's not that hard to do and easy to overdo out of negativity and powerlessness.

You don't owe it to anyone to say that you want to do what you don't want to do. Keep this simple, everyday business, not an act of defiance.

Are you getting uncomfortable as you think of applying this?

Does saying no seem anything but simple?

If saying no seems so difficult, it is probably because you have said yes so long and so insincerely that now you feel to say no will require explaining your previous deceptions and correcting them.

Even if this is true, it is a problem that will never go away until you begin to say what you really mean.

Say no and let it be the other person's problem.

❧

How I feel is enough to know what I want.

Say Yes

Yes!
What power this word has.

"Do you love me?"

"Yes!"

"Did I do a good job?"

"Yes!"

If you want to hear yes, you need to say yes.

Saying yes is a sign of power, confidence, knowledge, and giving.

Yes is what love is about.

Yes is about commitment and knowing the value of things.

Yes protects and claims, nourishes and revitalizes.

Yes is a smile, a supporting glance, a nod of agreement when others are withholding. Yes is a pat on the back. Yes is generosity itself.

Yes is the building block of kingdoms, the heart of religion, and the essence of being successful in business. In business anyone can say no; it takes someone with real power to say yes.

Say yes. Don't be afraid.

Say yes. You can do it.

Say yes. Claim your place. Find yourself. Celebrate lasting love. Build a family. Run the company. Write the novel. Overcome your weakness. Develop your strength. Test your specialness, and be master of your own world.

Yes. Yes. Yes.

❧

**I embrace my life
and find my life embracing me.**

Seek Your Best

❧

S earch out your strength, even when you doubt that it is there.

Especially when you doubt it is there.

Your strength hides in time of weakness and needs your belief to show itself.

Follow what you believe is right. You have no stronger guide than this belief. All other advice is approximate.

In time of need, your belief is your strength. What others believe does not make the long night any shorter.

Don't be disappointed by the shortcomings that you discover on your quest. Your knowledge of your shortcomings is as important as knowing your strength. When you know your weaknesses, you know what to look out for. You know how you will get in your own way.

Seek. Don't just sit there waiting for the world to present opportunities to you. The world is ignorant and is destined to ignore you if you do not act.

Create opportunities by believing in your best. The caring you show in the pursuit of your best creates a caring world around you.

Give your best a place in your life. If there is no room for your best, create it. Your best expands and needs to breathe.

Feelings are the breath of the soul. Make room for them by being truthful, simple, and loving.

Where will you find your best? Right in front of you, where it has always been.

What will your best say to you
when you find it?

"I am good; yes, I am good."

I am my strength.
I am not afraid to look within.

Being Alone

When you have found yourself, being alone is a privilege, not a punishment.

All the good work that you do comes when you are alone.

All your dreams are dreamed alone.

Your best ideas are conceived in solitude.

Your dream of a better world and the contribution you will make to it will also come when you are alone.

Your creations and inventions, your solutions to the problems that most vex you, all come to you in isolation.

It is only when you are by yourself that you can be receptive to the stillness of your inner voice.

This is the voice that tells you what you need to know, the inner directive, the heart of your soul given words.

This solitude is the place from which your originality and specialness issue.

In your aloneness you hear music and see art most clearly. Only when you are alone can you receive the gifts the world presents.

In your aloneness you are in touch with the energy that runs the world.

It is the place where God speaks to you and where you become God.

The things you take from this place fortify your spirit with grace, forgive your ineptness, and fill you with new resolve.

Learn to love being with yourself. It is the highest place to which you can aspire.

🐾

The good I've done rewards me in
solitude.
I find relief in being alone.
Here, I am at peace.

Share Your
Aloneness

Sharing your solitary self takes trust. Revealing the inner workings of your heart exposes you to the rebuke of indifference and the icy frustration of not being taken seriously.

Who wants to suffer the pain of not being heard when you most need someone to listen?

To allow another (it will only be one or two at best, never others) to come close, to know the same self you are when you are alone with yourself, is the heart of intimacy.

Being intimate is displaying in the presence of another the self you discover in solitude.

What a risk hangs on this.

If you show your true self and are rejected because the other person did not understand or care enough to allow you to make yourself understood, you recoil, perceiving the whole world as hollow, empty as a shadow play.

Where is life's meaning if such sacred knowing cannot be shared?

Kindred spirits do not need to work at this. In each other's presence they find all the encouragement they need to be alone together.

First you must love being alone with yourself.

Then you must love the other.

The selves that appear in that interface define a world that appears every time they are together.

Which is the reflection? Which is the source?

🍂

There is nothing between me and
myself.
The space is empty.
There is room here for one more
empty space, one more open person.
If I find that person, how wonderful.
If I don't, I am still with me.

Now

❧

Surrender to this moment.

This moment is the stuff of life.

Memories are past, both the good and the bad.

Fears define events that have not yet happened, and worry drives away simply being.

Live in this moment, at this time, when life takes place.

It will not take place. It has not taken place. It *is* taking place.

The being here, the being alive, and the am of "I am" are all happening now.

Now is never and forever, both fleeting and eternal.

Now is the gift of life spreading its wings in glad bestowal.

Now is now.

If you live for this moment, you live in every other part of time.

If you live in the past, you are not alive now. Unmourned sadnesses taint the joy of birdsong as memory recalls absent others, a recollection diminishing the self.

If you fear the future, the moment is infected with suspicion as you seek out the harbingers of doom in trivial disappointments.

Now is everything, but it is also nothing. It is none of the past and yet it is all of the past, the tip of the spear of time needing everything that led up to this moment to be itself.

Ride the moment bravely and in passion. It is where you are most alive. It is where children play and where silence fills the forest.

There is as much room in this moment as you are empty of your past.

❧

I am in this moment being me.

Move On

❧

What's the point of staying in that rut?

Are you getting comfortable with your misfortune?

Are you gathering your strength, waiting for another try?

Are you displaying your misfortune, feeling sorry for yourself?

Are you using your sad position as a convenient reason to complain to someone else?

Are you failing in order to disappoint another person? Do you think that other person notices? Do you think that other person should care?

Who should care about you when you don't care enough about yourself to lift yourself out of your dilemma?

Maybe you have to be in this rut in

order to convince yourself that you need to do something about it. After all, you've been there awhile and nothing much seems to have changed by itself.

OK, admit that things have gotten as bad as you say they have.

How long are you planning to suffer?

How much additional punishment do you think you deserve?

Call when you're ready to move on. It's always up to you.

Or maybe don't call, just move.

🐾

I am not attached to my past.
It lies behind me, a distant shore.
I am not attached to the world.
I glide over its surface.
I release all holds to hold onto me.
Having myself, I am safe.
I am free.

Be Patient

❧

There's really no point telling you to be patient.

You can only be patient if you feel you are on the right road.

The wrong road always makes you a little crazy. No matter how fast you travel, you're going nowhere until you abandon it.

You cannot be patient when you think you are wasting your life.

You know you should always be doing something else.

You can't even enjoy a vacation when you haven't found yourself, for you can't tell the difference between a vacation and the rest of your life. Nothing is happening in either place.

When you know where you are going you can do nothing and still be patient. You can take time out to enjoy yourself because you know you are going in the right direction when you are ready.

Adolescents are impatient all the time. They run from one party to the next, from one group of friends to another, always looking for excitement.

Purpose is patience.

You look for excitement when your life has no real meaning of its own.

If you can't relax, maybe you should start looking for the right goal, your goal, your destiny. Your impatience is telling you that time is running out and that you're wasting your life.

Be patient about everything else, but be impatient about finding your life.

"Be patient." These are empty words to a life empty of purpose.

When you find your purpose, no one will need to tell you to be patient.

❦

I seek the right road.
Finding it, I lose my doubts.
Traveling on it, I find my strength.
The road is my only goal.
I follow where it takes me.

Don't Let Your
Loneliness Run
Your Life

◆

If you want a recipe for disaster, let your loneliness motivate your choices. Choose to be with someone just because you're lonely.

The desperation that loneliness creates blinds you to the other person. You choose someone merely because that person stays with you.

It could just as well be a hundred other people when you choose the wrong person.

Any person can end your loneliness at first, but only the right person can keep you from missing yourself. The wrong person drives your best away.

You are never more lonely than

when you yearn to be your best.

When you are not your best, the times you spend by yourself are also times away from yourself. You are not what you want to be and you feel alienated from your journey and weary of the road.

And when you are with others, you use their presence like a drug. You need them too much. You fear their withdrawal and the abstinence of silence. In the middle of togetherness you anticipate parting and the fretful time when you will be alone with a self you do not esteem.

You need to tolerate your loneliness by knowing what it stands for.

See your loneliness as your heart's dream for a life filled with meaning.

Use your time alone to think about your passion.

Use your time to weave the fabric of your intention.

In the silence, find the echo of your true intent.

Be grateful for being alone.

Your loneliness is always for you.

❧

I live in the spaces between my thoughts.

Apologize

❧

Y ou can do it.
You've been feeling bad about it long enough.

If you INSIST you won't apologize, what do you think your determination is saying?

Perhaps that you were right or that the other person deserved it, but mostly you are just trying to convince yourself that what you did wasn't so hurtful.

So when you refuse to apologize, you're really trying to convince yourself that you are not bad.

Here's some news for you. Only strong, healthy people apologize.

You are not bad, even if you acted badly.

You are not bad, even if you acted badly *intentionally*.

You were probably hurt yourself, and your hurting was just the tip of the iceberg of your own anger.

Apologize, and also explain how you were hurt.

Take responsibility for the hurt that you caused and don't try to talk your way out of it.

Don't use your own hurt to justify being insensitive.

Be sincere.

Admit that you are only human.

Apologize.

You'll feel like yourself again.

I am good and always have something to give.

Expect a Positive Outcome

Since you are good, doing good fulfills you.

Your destiny is paved with acts of goodness.

Only the good feel guilty.

Only the angry feel self-pity.

Don't regret your failures, move on along the road.

Find reasons to like yourself and the world will follow.

You can risk and lose everything and still be your best.

You are not the center of the world; you *are* the world.

Expect a good result. Your expectations will create it.

I have the power to save myself.

Understand Your
Anger

❧

Anger is the memory of being hurt. Being angry is just proof that you didn't complete the job of expressing your hurt when it first occurred.

You're responsible for speaking your feelings, but expressing anger is always a problem. It's hard to express anger without hurting someone else. The best way to express anger is to show your hurt.

To resolve your anger, first possess your hurt. It's hard to admit that you've been hurt when you try to portray yourself as invincible or above it all.

If you push away your feelings to protect yourself, you become less real, less connected to your best. Even if you conceal your pain, you still act hurt and angry. You become sensitive to hurt and you seem irritable with others. Your hidden feelings speak indirectly.

Protecting another person from your hurt and angry feelings is just another way of alienating them. The longer you protect them, the more alienated you will feel.

After a while you won't feel joy in the right places, and when others ask what is wrong, you won't even be able to begin to tell them. It will seem like such a complicated old story.

People who hurt you and then prevent you from expressing that hurt damage you the most.

Anyone who can bottle up your anger can control you.

You need to be free of anger to love.

When love is coated with anger, it doesn't feel like love.

When anger is coated with love, it still feels like anger.

Express your hurt at the correct time and place and you'll always be free to love.

❧

My hurt is on my lips.
My love will follow.

When You Are
Competitive

❦

You compete with others when you find it difficult to define your own worth.

You find it easier to beat another than to be your best.

You are most competitive when you fear testing yourself.

When you compete, your actions come from envy and insecurity rather than from free choice.

You need to be first.

You need to win.

It doesn't matter at what, just so long as you are on top and people look up to you.

The problem with being competitive is that it always involves an audience, even if it is just one other person. Praise matters more than substance.

You always need someone else to beat or to please because pleasing yourself either isn't good enough or you don't believe it is possible.

You can only win playing to an audience of one, the part of you that knows what you want.

No truly great creative accomplishment was made out of the need to compete with another person.

All the world's greatness comes from individuals pleasing themselves.

When you please yourself, your triumph lasts only a moment, because the courage of your success immediately leads you on to test your worth again.

Competitive people may win, but they never really grow until they act for themselves.

❧

**I am here as myself.
I have already won.**

You Don't Need
Permission

❧

Whose permission are you looking for, anyway?

What if the other person gives you permission?

What if the other person withholds approval?

What difference does it make?

Permission is what the people in control demand of riskers.

The people whose permission you are seeking want you to ask for permission because their approval is the only thing they have to give.

People who have lost the drive for individual achievement, but still want power, withhold approval the most. They are the hardest to convince, and they believe in the old ways and theories long after they have been shown to be false.

The people who need permission the most are people who don't trust themselves.

Just for the record: If permission were needed, there would have been no innovation in art, no discovery in science, no social advancement, and no justice.

The innovator and creator are always denigrated for breaking free.

Live your life and take the risks that you need to take to get where you need to go.

Don't expect other people to understand or approve.

When you go out on your own, others will be more concerned about

the rules you broke than the excellence
of what you accomplished.

Permission granted.

🐘

I believe in my goodness.
I trust my intentions.
I follow the bidding of my heart.

Remember Your
Strength

❧

You are as strong as your greatest
strength.

You are always stronger than your
weaknesses.

Your strength is always real.

You are never weaker than your
strength.

Only you sometimes forget.

❧

I am my goodness.
I am all my goodness.
Even when I feel I am less,
I am always more.

Speak Up

❧

Speak up against lies, injustice, cruelty, and evil.

Most of the time you do not personally encounter such grave affronts.

The trespasses against you and those you love only take on this perspective of enormity when you delay speaking up to them.

The evil that lives in your world has more to do with the pain you withhold and your failure to assert yourself than with the maliciousness of others.

After a while your unexpressed hurt makes you feel as if the world is against you and transforms harmless oversights into dark affronts.

Speak out against little trespasses or you cede your emotional territory.

Speak out against the harm done

to you or you encourage it to continue.

Just speak out in time and be clear in expressing yourself. You don't need to take arms and go to war to redress your personal grievances.

If you did, your actions would be seen as hostile, not defensive, and never justifiable, no matter how good a cause you had or how deeply hurt you felt.

You don't need much language if your heart is open.

It is your silence that empowers the evil you encounter.

🍂

I listen and hear my voice.
I speak the words of my experience.
I tell my dreams.
I share my truth.

Crazy

❧

Being crazy is holding onto pain.
The greater the time elapsed between the hurt and expressing it, the crazier you are.

Unforgiven hurt fuels angry fantasies that make you doubt yourself and infect your thinking with unspeakable retaliation, bad dreams, and an uneasiness of the soul.

You feel especially crazy when you doubt your goodness, for then you're always lost and the center of your life no longer holds.

The time you seem craziest to others is when you vacillate before making a decision.

Crazy is being torn between two masters, two conflicting ideals.

"Can I be for myself without alienating you and risk losing your love?"

You never feel more crazy than when people lie to you.

And when people lie about loving you, they hurt you the most.

Being crazy is not knowing what to believe.

There is no imprisonment worse than being bound to a crazy person, for then you can only be real by paying a price.

The way to become crazy is to try to please everyone all the time.

The only freedom from craziness is telling the truth.

❧

Only my voice can tell my truth.
Only my truth can heal my world.

Success

❧

Success is liking how you feel about what you do.

Any success makes you feel successful when you accept yourself.

When you don't, nothing makes a difference.

Where your passion lies, there too lies your success. So do your best at what makes you happy.

No one can ask more, and you won't be satisfied with less.

Success is a lonely place, because true success is mastery over yourself. You climb to the top of your talent and survey the world through your own eyes. No one can share your perspective. No one's praise means much, but anyone's criticism can touch you, for success makes you open to the slightest weakness in yourself.

You realize that to win the greatest success, you don't use power, but your vulnerability, for true success makes you humble.

And you come to understand that only if you can fail well can you succeed.

When you succeed, you know that failure, like success, is always just behind the next door.

The only true failure is fearing to risk.

**I accept everything that brought me
to this place.
I am open to criticism.
I intend to grow.**

Intimacy

&

Feelings are the language of the heart.

The feelings you share determine the quality of your relationship.

If you cannot tell your feelings, your relationship is empty, distant, a figment of your hope, too fragile to trust in dark times.

It is your love that motivates you to be together.

It is your pain that obliges you to share.

And it is the remembrance of your joy together that gives you the courage to risk being open.

A loving heart cannot bear isolation.

When you share your feelings, you are least alone.

The feelings you withhold also limit the love you can express.

If you conceal your hurt, you forget your love.

If you lie about your anger, you cannot tell if your love is real.

Your feelings have to be heard in order for them to be fully expressed.

Ask to be heard and speak plainly.

Share your painful feelings and be free to love once more.

❧

I admit my pain and sorrow in order
to know joy.
I believe in my strength in order to
find it.

The Wisdom of Feelings

❧

In feelings there is wisdom, for the simplest feelings speak the greatest truth.

Pain in life comes from avoiding the truth that your feelings tell.

Any road that avoids feelings cannot be right.

Hiding from your feelings only makes you go in circles.

Become comfortable with your feelings, because your feelings are your life.

Trust your feelings. They're the only true guidance you'll ever get.

If you know what you're feeling, you know what the world is revealing to you.

If you cannot be true to your feelings, you cannot be true to yourself.

Trust your feelings, but first you have to know what you really feel.

When you find out when a feeling started, you also find out why.

The feelings you are afraid to release cause you to hold onto other things.

Stay up-to-date with your feelings. Don't store them. When a feeling ages, it becomes less honest.

The more immediately you express your hurt, the more completely it resolves.

Stand up for your feelings and you're free to be yourself.

You have to be able to cry to live fully, for tears in the right place cause healing.

Your feelings are explanation enough. Let them speak.

The greatest credential is the human heart.

❧

I face myself.
I see myself.
I know myself.
I welcome my best self into my life.

When Feelings Go Astray

●

You can never put your heart away without losing yourself.

When you hide from your feelings, you hide from your life.

More pain is caused from hiding the truth than from anything else.

You've got to make peace with your feelings in order to catch up with your life, for the difficulty you have in expressing your feelings becomes the hard life you live.

Hurt that is buried often becomes anger directed at yourself.

The angry feelings you fear expressing become dark thoughts that plague you.

When feelings are withheld, it is

easy to confuse guilt with love and ob-ligation with preference.

The strength you feel comes from the truth you tell about the way you feel.

You need to be strong to feel safe enough to cry.

When you close down your feel-ings, you only widen your exposure to pain.

Feel your pain and your life will open up again.

❧

I am everything I experience,
and yet I am always good.
I am everything I feel,
and always have love to give.

Give

🖤

A happy directive it is that prompts you to love.

Give.

And become your own source.

The goodness you feel comes from the goodness you give.

Put out good and you become better.

Give, and your giving defines you.

In times of confusion and self-doubt, your giving is a light.

The best way to get your mind off yourself is to give.

When you give to other people you lose your own pain.

Give what you would like to receive, but don't expect anything in return. Whatever you expect only shapes your future disappointment.

Give your appreciation, under-standing, support, and love, but from strength.

Giving out of weakness is merely a form of begging.

What you give to yourself cannot be taken away.

What you give to others is your gift to yourself.

Give from the heart and it will fill the world.

When you reach out to touch the world, the giving part of you fills all your needy places.

Give.

And grow full.

🐾

**When I am in doubt, I must
remember to give.**

Growing

You're here to grow into your best. You need to be free to grow, to have the emotional room to breathe, to stretch and try your wings, to succeed, and, especially, to fail.

There are no rules to guide you. You need to find your own way, at your own pace, and to accept the truths you discover about yourself.

You have to give up your safety net and risk. You'll discover that your world grows with the mistakes you can take responsibility for.

If you allow your parents to stay too close, you remain a child forever. You cannot grow in the presence of a parent who does not believe that you are good.

You cannot grow if you are always protected.

Growing is freeing the good that is already there. You do this by letting go of what does not work for you. The loss of a false fantasy is a gain, but you have to find this out for yourself.

You grow most when you live in the belief that you have something to give to the world.

If you don't grow, everything becomes a repetition of the past.

You always grow when you give your love.

The self you admire is the person you become.

Failure to admit the truth always blocks your growth, and even fools and children have lessons to teach.

Don't grow old, grow better.

To expect to grow is to stay forever young.

🐦

I let go of doubt.
I free myself.
I embrace the new.
I find myself again.

Don't Suffer

❧

Everyone who suffers is a little bit unrealistic.

Suffering is mostly about events that have already happened, and much suffering is about events that happened long ago.

You were not put here to suffer. It just sometimes feels that way.

You suffer when you keep pain alive, for smoldering pain continually creates anger. These smothered feelings live inside you, hurting you because they have no place to go.

When you cannot own your tears, you lose yourself.

When you cannot mourn, you suffer.

You suffer as long as you hold false beliefs.

You suffer when you cannot forgive.

No one suffers like the proud, for they have to pretend that they were not hurt. Their joy becomes brittle.

No one's suffering is more bitter than that of controlling people, for they suffer in isolation.

No one suffers more desperately than dependent people, for they cannot let go.

Accept what has happened.

Learn your lessons.

Mourn your losses.

And release.

Grief knows no clock, and suffering can swallow up your life.

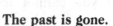

The past is gone.
I cannot call it back.

How You See
the World

❧

Is the water glass half-full?
  Or is it half-empty?
  Are you an optimist?
  Or are you a pessimist?
  Both answers are wrong, because each is biased.

  The correct answer is that the glass contains water.

  The same amount of water would be overlooked in a barrel and overflow a thimble. What is the point?

  You perceive the world in relative terms because you grew up in relationship to other people. Your family had more or less than other families, and you complained that a sibling was treated better because he or she got more. More meant good. Less meant bad.

Reality is not relative, but the way you see it is.

If you feel rejected and at the bottom of life's ladder, you find evidence wherever you look that the world is a dark and hopeless place. And you are wrong.

When you have triumphed and found love, been promoted to the coveted position, and are celebrated in the press, you think the world is a place of unlimited possibility and wonder. And you are just as wrong.

The world is neither good nor bad.

It simply is.

You, too, have the potential to be good and bad.

Cherish your good and build upon it. Neither ignore your weakness nor despise it.

Live in the empty and full part of your life at the same time.

❧

In accepting everything, I find myself.

The Next Step

❧

Wherever you're going, whatever your dreams, the next step you take will be from this place.

You cannot take that next step unless you know where you are right now.

To risk without knowing the ground you stand upon is to leap into the darkness.

The next step is not going to be all that different from the steps you took to get to this place.

Know this place. Know how you got here, your motivations, the truth about your shortcomings, the limitations that held you back.

Know the ground on which you stand, without illusion, pretense, or self-deception.

We all want to believe we are better

off than we are, but at the time when we risk and have to look into the depth of the chasm we're trying to span, our weaknesses display themselves and deflate our resolve.

So know where you are. Accept your condition for what it is. Take responsibility for getting here and staying as long as you have.

If you've been stuck, admit your fear and lack of courage. Don't blame others. Don't condemn the world.

The place where you stand is the consequence of your determination. If you find your achievements lacking, look to yourself, not outside.

Perhaps you were not motivated. Perhaps you did not want what you claimed you needed. Perhaps you only fooled yourself.

If you understand how you got to

this place, you will know the next step and how to take it.

Don't fear the future, read the past.

✎

There is nothing beneath me; I am not afraid.
There is nothing above me; I still believe.
I know that wherever I land, it will be as me, moving forward.

Reflection

L ife is what you make of it.
There are no rules.

If you live honestly, you learn about life.

When you hide from yourself, the world escapes in the shadows, for then you see only the parts that agree with you.

Life is not difficult when you live in the truth.

For most of your difficulties are disputes with what is.

Don't take the world so personally.

It merely reflects you.

It's not out to get you.

Do your best, but be your own judge.

When you try too hard, you miss life.

Follow your love, not your doubt.

In your life it is always time to flourish.

I remember my dream of my best, and live it until it comes true.

Unreasonable
People

❧

Your strength is in doing what you believe is right and not concerning yourself with other people's responses.

Unreasonable people gain their power from the way you react to them.

You don't even have to agree with them to give them power. You just have to react.

The child who is teased the most is the one who makes the biggest protest.

Children tease other children not because they are evil but because they feel powerless. Getting a response from a weaker person gives them a feeling of strength.

All of the unreasonable people you meet gain their power from your response.

When you respond to an unreasonable person by getting emotional, you give them victory.

How do you manage unreasonable people?

You dismiss them.

Like teasing.

Like shadows.

❧

I bend with the wind.
I glide with the current.
I do not resist—I remain myself.

Take the Time to
Do Nothing

❧

Time for gathering your thoughts.
Time for feeling the sun.

Time for listening to the sounds of nature.

Too many events fill your day, crowd you out of your life, and leave you exhausted without a clear recollection of what you did.

If you paused and took time to put expectations and schedules aside and took a walk instead of lunch, you'd remember that time, empty of intention, more clearly than your busy day.

It is in the empty spaces that life takes place—not in the planning, but in the repose.

You need to be present for what is not there as much as you are for what is.

You need to sense the volume of things.

The expanse of sky.

The breadth of horizon.

You are measured by the things you see.

Your contemplation shapes your life as much as your doing.

Be more on the edge, where looking out and looking in meet.

All truth gathers there and defines your being.

♠

I experience everything.
I hold onto nothing.
I become the world.

Hear Your Own Voice

❧

Listen.
    Stop.
Listen.
Inside there is an answer.
What does it say?
Inside there is a voice.
Whom does it serve?
You are the direction.
You are the force.
You are the reason.
Listen.
Shh.
Listen.
Find yourself.

❧

**I am in touch with the knowing that
is being alive.**

Know Yourself

You are the sum total of everything you did, thought, said, dreamed, avoided, embraced, abandoned, disputed, suffered, felt, expressed, withheld, promised, lost, gained, owned, borrowed, inherited, stole, needed, and loved.

There is no avoiding yourself.

You are all the good.

All the bad.

The times spent in joyous rapture.

The days of mourning and lamentation.

You are your soul.

Your body is just a vessel—abused by self-deception and wearing the telling marks of indifferent upkeep, reflecting your resistance to accepting and knowing yourself.

What use is it to dispute what everyone else knows?

What is to be gained by denying what you know in your heart?

You are as good as you are and your faults are plenty.

Come, accept yourself.

The day is still young and there is time yet to play.

❧

I am all of me.
Nothing is missing.

Save Yourself

✦

J ust in case you were not sure of what you are supposed to do during this incarnation, this is a reminder.

Save yourself.

That's the reason for your being here.

That's why you have feelings—to save yourself.

Your fear warns you of danger.

Your hurt tells you to get out of the line of fire.

Your anger energizes your defenses.

But sometimes you ignore them.

You stay in situations where you feel threatened because you put other people's feelings first.

You bury your hurt because you doubt yourself and are afraid that you will suffer even more if you speak out.

You turn your anger against yourself because you are unwilling to take a stand.

You were placed inside you to save yourself.

Don't wait for help.

Help yourself.

Don't cry to be rescued.

Climb to safety.

You don't need to make a case.

Just trust your feelings and follow them.

I look both ways before crossing.
I cross to the other side.

Trust Yourself

❦

Everything starts with trusting yourself.

If you don't trust yourself, who should?

If you don't trust yourself, whose support will make any difference?

Trust that your idea is good.

Trust that your feeling is real.

Trust that your judgment is correct.

Trust that you want what you want.

Trust that what makes you happy makes you happy.

Life is not supposed to be complicated, a long, drawn-out debate about its meaning and how you fit into the scheme of things.

You are the scheme of things.

You are life.

Your doubt removes you from yourself.

Trusting yourself doesn't mean that you're always going to be right.

It just allows you to overcome your doubt and correct your mistakes.

Trusting yourself doesn't mean that you're perfect, but that you are perfectly willing to be human.

All the good that you intend needs your trust to energize it and make it come to pass.

Without trust, your dreams languish and soon hope itself dies.

You can doubt anything you want.

But for the moment trust yourself and fill your life.

I am just where I have placed myself.
I can move.
I can stay.
All I need is to know my heart
and follow it.

What Do You Know?

❧

Most of what you believe is based on hearsay, gossip, and distortion.

The facts take years to sift.

Reality boils. It is not a millpond. Its roiling surface is opaque with the confused seas of the moment. Its contents are the mystery we must navigate through and inhabit.

Time is sedentary, sorting by gravity what is important from the dust of experience. You can never know the full meaning of your life in your own time. Perhaps you should be less harsh on yourself.

You can never know your past completely, for remembering is a distortion itself.

Your childhood, both the deprivation and the innocent wonder, the betrayal and the promise, are seen through the flawed glass of your needs.

You invent your history by selecting what you choose to remember and what you allow to remain hidden.

Even when your knowing is dim, persisting only in remnant attitudes or hidden fears, what you know still reflects everything you have experienced.

You are your memory, large and small, retained in your character, body, and being.

Some part of your past is always telling on you.

Awaken from the dream of innocence and remember your history.

Know how you color the world.

True freedom is openness to your past.

❧

I am a reflection of my memory.
I am substance, I am real.
I am the world passing.
I am the world about to be born.

Let Others Be Free

❧

L et other people be free.
        Free to accept you, free to
turn you away.

Let other people be free to love
you and to love you not.

If these words strike your heart
with the agony of anticipated rejection,
consider for a moment that only people
who are free not to love you can love
you completely.

Love can only be given freely, for
the slightest obligation dulls passion.

Let other people be free.

Free to embrace your ideas, free to
dispute them with enthusiasm.

The people who are your strongest
allies support you because they believe
in you, not because they fear you. The

coerced supporter is merely an enemy waiting to come to full strength.

People are loyal to the person who allows them to be free.

People support the person who respects their independence.

Democracies do not fight each other; neither do people who are free.

Trying to control others only makes them resist.

When you try to control others, you waste your energy and squander your resources. It's like trying to contain the wind.

When you try to control others, you always lose your own freedom.

🍂

I release my grip, so that my intention is free to take me where it will.

Don't Be Afraid to Dream

❧

Your dream is the infancy of your gift.

Your belief in your dream makes it a reality.

Abandon yourself to your dream. Let go.

Dream the dream that has been within you forever.

Be the child in your dreams.

Value closeness.

Play with light.

Lose yourself in your senses, and see the world anew.

Be the hero in your dreams.

Save the nations.

Bridge the flood.

Conquer evil.

Build the peace.

The world needs your dreams.
Carry them forward.
You are your dreams.
Claim and deliver them.
You find yourself by living your dream.

**Let me dream my life,
but let me not dream my life away.**

Don't Make
Excuses

❦

When you make excuses, no one really believes you.

As a matter of fact, if you don't want to be taken seriously, make excuses for your mistakes instead of admitting them.

An excuse is like a red flag.

When you make an excuse, you change your tone of voice and your posture. You try too hard to convince others of what they already know is false.

When you make an excuse, you are practically shouting, "Look at me, everyone, I'm lying."

Of course you don't see it that way, for making excuses blinds you.

You want to believe in the excuse. You don't want to be wrong.

So what if you are wrong?

No one cares.

But people do care when you make excuses, because in every excuse is blame, putting it off on someone else, usually the person you are making excuses to.

They don't like that.

Anything, no matter how small or ridiculous, will serve as an excuse if you don't want to take responsibility for your actions.

It's much better to admit what everyone else knows is so and get on with your business.

There are no excuses that will ease the pain of failing to do what you're supposed to do in this life.

❧

My life is the answer.
I seek to define the question.

Expectations

❧

Your expectations rob you of joy more than your failures do.

Expectations create disappointment in the middle of success by allowing you to feel that, because good is not great, it is not good at all.

The expectation of failure is failure.

When you expect to lose, you hunt for the signs of loss and react to them as proof of your failure, missing success in the process.

If you don't expect anything, withholding people will not disappoint you.

If you expect too much, even giving people will let you down.

It is a difficult balance to attain, being open and being alert.

You want to experience life's joys without being suspicious or jaded.

And you don't want to be hurt.

Innocence doesn't anticipate deceit.

That is why children can be so blissful.

Still, like everyone else, you learn that even the best plans can go amiss and that the love you once believed would last forever can fade.

There's no surprise as shocking as discovering something you never expected to face.

You need to protect yourself without diminishing your openness.

The sting of betrayal is in the innocence it destroys.

Lowering your expectations raises your integrity.

❧

**Everything makes sense.
But only good makes it right.**

Trust Your
Experience

❧

No one knows the road you've traveled but you.

Where you stand, no one else has ever stood before.

Where you will step is always new, even if you tread on the footprints of others.

For you bring your history into each new moment, shading it with a meaning and perspective that makes it your own.

What other people say is always from their perspective.

Your truth lies between your experience and your memory.

You are always defining your way.

Your experience is your only teacher and true directive, providing you accept it all, the good and the bad.

If you know the sea, you know storms.

If you know your experience, the future will not surprise you.

🐾

Let me remember the path—the steps, the stones, the resting places.
I have been here before.
I will be here again.

Take Charge

Take charge and acquire the power you've been yearning for.

Be the judge of what's right for you.

Validate yourself.

Don't wait for praise.

Accept that the problems you create are the most difficult ones to solve.

Solve them anyhow.

Admit your mistakes and correct them.

Admit your distortions and live honestly.

Whenever you're blocked, express yourself.

Believe in your worth and act on that belief.

Take responsibility for the triumph and the tragedy.

The love lost, the love won.

Take responsibility for everything
in your life.
It's the price of freedom.

❧

**Even when I forget,
I am free to hold on.
I am free to let go.
I am free to choose my own way.**

Fix Your Problems

All lives have chapters in trouble.
But everyone's hell is different.

No one knows what you're going through.

No one can judge how badly you hurt.

You cannot convey how it feels to live with your troubles.

Sometimes you can't even admit it to yourself.

The problems you contain confine you, dull your senses, numbing you, making it easier not to care and to sink into helplessness.

Don't run.

Don't panic.

Face the situation.

Just believe you can do it.

When something goes wrong, fix it as soon as you can.

When you are in pain, express it, just as you feel it.

When a misunderstanding occurs, discuss it when the question is fresh in everyone's mind.

When an unfairness takes place, dispute it as it is happening.

When a problem occurs, work on it.

The best time is now.

The right person is you.

❧

It's just another day.
It's just another time.
I tell my story by living it.

Too Close for
Comfort

❧

You almost lost everything.
But the car stayed on the road.

The deal came through.

Your loved one pulled through!

You got a second chance.

You feel relief when you feel safe.

The danger is past; now you can think about what almost happened.

You put your false bravery aside. Perhaps you didn't even know you were at risk. Perhaps you didn't know what really mattered.

Your relief always reflects a hidden fear.

Your relief measures your fear and denial.

Perhaps you had too much at stake to face it all at once.

When you were in danger, you had to protect yourself by minimizing your risk.

Now you lower your defenses and can look at reality without pretending.

You can admit how much losing really meant to you.

Relief is the beginning of self-knowledge.

Relief lets you feel your attachments and know how much you care.

Knowing what you really love is finding your strength.

I study my relief and discover myself.

Rescuing

❦

You cannot rescue the world.

You cannot save yourself by saving someone else.

Rescuing others only postpones their learning the lesson they need to grow.

When you rescue people, you also undermine them.

They're grateful at first, but later on resent you for making them admit they were unable to save themselves.

The greater the rescue, the deeper the resentment.

It's not what you were thinking when you offered your help.

If the gift you give is of yourself, such as your understanding and kindness, that is one matter, for such gifts are encouragements to others to risk for themselves.

However, a gift of money has a double edge. There are always strings attached.

Money imprisons the receiver in obligation and self-doubt.

Money makes the giver feel superior, powerful, and expectant. The reason you rescue others is not out of kindness, but weakness. You are trying to buy affection.

It always turns out badly.

Rescue your friend and you'll lose him or her.

Rescue your partner and destroy your love.

Rescue your children and you'll cripple them.

When you rescue others, you're always blamed when something goes wrong and you lose what affection they once had for you.

❦

My freedom depends on letting others be free.

Understanding
Your Anxiety

❧

Anxiety speaks danger's tongue and warns of approaching hurt.

Most anxiety comes from deceiving yourself, for you fear most what you will not examine.

Hide from the truth and your life becomes full of worry.

When you are in darkness, it is easy to imagine the worst, for in darkness there is only the unknown.

You cannot get rid of the anxiety you play down. Soon it takes you over, for fear spreads when you conceal it. When you won't face what you fear, you have to cover everything to be safe.

An anxious mind doesn't solve problems, it only creates more, for anxiety has a way of filling up all the spaces where you dream and reason. When you are anxious, you always fall behind.

You can always summon up your fears. An anxious person always finds something to worry about.

Admit the truth and your anxiety will begin to subside.

If you know where your anxiety began, you know how to end it. You can make a plan to protect and save yourself.

You have to remember your strength to find it.

Make your wants greater than your fears.

You empower your fear by doubting yourself.

Name the fear, then conquer!

Feel your fear and do what you have to do.

My fear helps focus my strength.
I defeat fear by believing in myself.

Be Your Best Self

Within you is an island of sanity, your best self.

It is a source of power, a reservoir of strength.

You find it only when you believe in yourself.

And you present it to others only when it is safe to tell the truth.

Choose to be with people who care about you, who bring out your best.

Your best self is found in acceptance, nurtured by simplicity, and maintained in vulnerability.

Loving yourself and telling the truth is being your best.

If you don't tell the truth, your best self eludes you.

When you live a life that is less than your best, you have less to give to the world.

When you are not your best, the world suffers because your presence is a drain.

Your best self starts sentences with the words "I love," "I understand," "I accept," "I forgive," and "I trust."

Your best is defined by giving.

Your best self is childlike, open-eyed with wonder, expecting to produce magic, but never looking to be delivered out of desperation.

Keep company with your best and be a friend to the world.

🖤

**I love my best self.
It's always there.**

Being Open

❧

L iving openly is best.
Anything that stands between
you and your heart creates pain.

Talking about problems is admitting you have them.

Admitting problems is the first
step in solving them.

You can't solve a problem you
won't face.

You can't be fixed if you don't reveal the part of you that's broken.

Hide even a small fault and it keeps
you from getting close.

Disclose a great weakness and you
create intimacy.

What you conceal becomes your
suffering.

Try to protect yourself against all
possible hurt and you hurt yourself

more than you would if you were open.

You can never be safe if you can never be happy.

The shield that protects against any hurt diminishes every joy.

If you stand up for your pain, you can love.

Love can only flourish where it is easy to tell the truth.

The world is about taking in, not shutting out.

Be open to all of you.

To love yourself, accept all of yourself.

No one is alone who loves himself or herself.

❧

I love myself.
I do not fear what lies inside me.
Therefore the world is not a mystery,
and I have a place to abide.

The Illusion of Being in Control

❦

You cannot control your life, you can only do what's right in each moment.

Your approach to the moments becomes your life.

What can you control that is really worth anything?

The best things are free, but you need to be free to enjoy them.

Love is either free or it is not love.

You have to be free to give and receive.

The feeling you try to control, controls you.

You cannot control others without losing their love.

If you protect someone else from pain, you destroy his or her motivation.

If you hold the upper hand over others, you cannot love them, you can only abuse them.

When you use anything but acceptance to get your way, you're only manipulating others.

You can't buy love without paying interest for the rest of your life.

When you have to pay for love, you're only controlled in return.

Release your grip.

Loosen your hold.

Let it all be.

Declare what you want.

Risk rejection and failure.

❧

I allow people to be what they are.
I can only be myself.

Courage

❧

C ourage is knowing the necessity of a thing.

So courage comes from facing reality.

Your strength comes from seeing the obstacle and reaching within for resolve.

Without the fear of failure your attention is not focused.

You need the danger to chastise you, to hold your interest, and to give the extra effort that completes you.

The extra effort is also you, but it needs to be stirred from reserves.

Wishful thinking is but a fool's way of gaining courage.

Bravery in fantasy, a cloistered virtue.

Telling people how they should live

their lives when your own is a mess, being a Monday-morning quarterback without ever taking the field, playing devil's advocate without having an original idea, these are all the occupations of cowards. And sometimes fools as well.

What matter if in your fantasy you picture yourself king, benevolent dictator, hero, and victor if in reality you cower at the approach of fools and cannot stand up for yourself in easy conversation?

The difference between such fantasy and rousing your courage from slumber is comparing escaping with being alive.

Anxiety is not for paralysis but preparation.

Life is for living, not discussing endlessly.

The unanalyzed life may not be

worth living, but the unlived life is
surely not worth analyzing.

❧

**I am always at the beginning of
discovering something wonderful
about myself.**

❧

About the Author

David Viscott, M.D., is an internation-
ally known psychiatrist and the author
of *The Language of Feelings*, *How to
Live with Another Person*, *Risking*,
and, most recently, *Emotionally Free*.
He is also an Emmy Award-winning
talk show host. Dr. Viscott lives in Los
Angeles.